* **

GET

* RICH *

AND STAY

* RICH *

STEP-BY-STEP INSTRUCTIONS FOR:

- HIGH SCHOOL STUDENTS -
- COLLEGE STUDENTS -
- ANYONE WHO WORKS FOR A LIVING –

NEW: EXPANDED STOCK MARKET COVERAGE

JOHN GILBERT BEAN

JohnGilbertBean.wordpress.com

***

Publisher's Cataloging-in-Publication

Bean, John Gilbert, 1933 –

GET RICH AND STAY RICH

/ Maureen Bean – ed.

    p. cm.

    Includes index

    1. Investing   2. Wealth

    3. Economics

    I. Title

ISBN-13: 978-1530959013
ISBN-10: 1530959012
Published by: John Gilbert Bean Publishing
       SAN: 253-0287

       951-461-4469
       Send comments to: JBeanMBean@msn.com

1st **EDITION April 13, 2016   REVISED May 13 ,2013   REVISED July 13, 2016**

CONTENTS

6. NO MATTER WHAT THE SELLER PROMISES, IF IT'S NOT WRITTEN IN THE CONTRACT, IT DOESN'T EXIST.

7. REAL-ESTATE "FLIPPING" HAS BECOME EPIDEMIC - PUT REAL-ESTATE AGENTS, FLIPPERS, AND OTHER PEOPLE'S MONEY TO WORK FOR YOU.

8. REAL ESTATE – PERSONAL RESIDENCE.

9. REAL ESTATE – RENTAL.

10. BUSINESS – GROW BY MERGER – BUT NEVER LOSE CONTROL!

11. INVESTING IN STOCK MARKET: STOCKS, MUTUAL FUNDS, AND EXCHANGE TRADED FUNDS (ETF).

11.1. STOCK IS CERTIFICATE OF SHARE OF OWNERSHIP OF COMPANY.

11.2. AS INVESTOR, YOUR GOAL SHOULD BE FOR EACH SHARE OF STOCK YOU OWN TO INCREASE IN VALUE BY AT LEAST 10 PERCENT EVERY YEAR.

11.3. INVESTING IN STOCKS OF SPECIFIC COMPANIES.

11.4. SELECTING STOCKS, MUTUAL FUNDS, AND EXCHANGE TRADED FUNDS (ETF).

11.5. INVESTING IN STOCKS FOR LONG TERM (15 - 30 YEARS).

11.6. INVESTING FOR SHORT TERM (5 - 10 YEARS).

11.7. COMMON MISTAKES MADE BY STOCK INVESTORS.

11.8. TYPICAL STOCK SYMBOLS, NAMES, AND ATTRIBUTES.

11.9. DEVELOP A DIVERSIFIED INVESTMENT PLAN FOR MAXIMUM RETURN AT MINIMUM RISK.

11.9.1. EXAMPLE 1 DIVERSIFICATION SUMMARY

11.9.2. EXAMPLE 2 DIVERSIFICATION SUMMARY

11.9.3. EXAMPLE INVESTMENT ACTON PLAN

11.9.4. DIVERSIFICATION SUMMARY WORKSHEET

11.9.5. INVESTMENT ACTION PLAN WORKSHEET

12. EPILOGUE. ENJOY YOUR WEALTH!

PREFACE.

Stop complaining and take action.
You are going to be dead a long time.

My Mother Clara was 41, my Father Frank Kirby Bean was 45 - when I was born at home in our house on the corner of Wadsworth Blvd and 32nd street in Edgewater (Denver), Colorado. Doctor Louis Gilbert delivered me, hence my middle name Gilbert. My birth date was March 13, 1933. The number 13 was very lucky (!) for me, which is why the publication date on my books is always 13th of the month of their publication. It is my goal that the information herein will be both lucky and valuable for the reader.

I have three older brothers now all deceased. Frank was 22 years older than me, Joe 18 years older, and Fred 3 years older.

My father died when I was 2, leaving my mother a widow and two small children just as the Great Depression of the 1920's and 1930's was ending thanks to the policies of President Franklin Roosevelt.   My Father was Construction Superintendent for the Colorado Bell Telephone Company – a very important job in Colorado winters when the huge snow storms in the Rocky Mountains knocked out telephone service lines throughout the state. There weren't any cell phones or internet then – just land lines on telephone poles. His job was to get all Colorado telephones back in service. Unfortunately, in a huge blizzard in 1935, he was working day and night and contracted pneumonia leading to his death.

Thus, in 1935, my Mother was left with two small boys, no pension, and no social security. She did what every mother does: **WHATEVER NECESSARY TO TAKE CARE OF HER CHILDREN.** Although my Mother never discussed the events with me, she married my Stepfather Elmo Parr in 1937 probably through a Lonely Hearts Club. Mom was 45, Elmo was 68. We then moved to Scottsbluff, Nebraska.

Elmo was a lifelong bachelor and a retired US Mail clerk working on the railroad route from Chicago to Omaha. Mail would be put on the train at each stop. Elmo sorted it and then delivered it to the appropriate city on the train's route. He never made much money but became wealthy by ruthlessly living frugally, saving his modest income, and investing in underpriced Nebraska farmland during the great depression.
Elmo had never been married and never had children. Suddenly having a family at age 68 with two head-strong young boys was a great shock to his lifestyle. Even though Elmo had plenty of money, we lived very, very frugally. Elmo had the money but never ate the cake (enjoyed his money).

So how did Elmo become RICH working at a low paying job? By observing Elmo, I learned what I have named **ELMO'S METHOD TO BECOME WEALTHY.** That's in **Section 2** of this book.
My Mother divorced Elmo when I was 12 years old because of friction between Elmo and my older brother Fred. Fortunately, I had received a bicycle for Christmas and was soon able to get a job delivering the daily newspaper for the Scottsbluff Nebraska Star Herald. I delivered newspapers every morning from 3 to 7 AM. I bought newspapers from the Star Herald and then collected from each of my individual route customers once a month.   I essentially owned my own business at age 14.

My first newspaper route had about 300 papers. Since I was a newcomer, my route was the most strung out - sometimes there were only one or two houses in a block. It was great in the summer – I would pedal my bike along the streets and sidewalks, and throw a folded newspaper like a Frisbee up to the front door of each house. I got to be very, very accurate. But in rain or winter snow storms, I had to get off my bike and walk each newspaper up to each house and put the newspaper inside the screen door so the it didn't get wet or snow didn't cover it.   The Blizzard of '49 was tough.

From that time on, I totally supported myself. I knew then that I could always take care of myself and my family.

PREFACE (CONTINUED).

From watching Elmo, I also learned that money doesn't bring happiness, There is more to being wealthy than just counting your money and assets. The complete picture includes:

- Accumulating wealth using Elmo's method.

- Increasing wealth.

- Keeping wealth.

- Enjoying wealth.

John Gilbert Bean
JohnGilbertBean.wordpress.com

Send comments to JBeanMBean@msn.com

GET RICH AND STAY RICH.

DEDICATION.

This work is dedicated to my wonderful wife, Maureen, who by her awesome goodness and talents gave me a taste of Paradise and the will to accomplish important things.
        JGB

ABOUT THE AUTHOR.

John Gilbert Bean has a BS Degree in Physics from the University of Arizona and graduate study in Physics and Electrical Engineering at the University of Arizona and California State University at Northridge (formerly San Fernando Valley State College). He served in the Marine Corps as a Radar Instructor.

As well as writing and teaching, his career spanned Engineering, Engineering Management, and Program Management responsible for design, development and integration of advanced systems at RCA, Hughes Aircraft, and Northrop Grumman.

His career and interests enabled him to work at the forefront of technology in the rapidly changing relevant science and mathematics of the origin and destiny of our Universe and Space beyond. He has written two other books: ***Communicating Successfully with Everyone*** and ***The Universe, Space, and Beyond.***

1.0. MEANING OF RICH.

1.1. HOW MUCH IS "RICH?"

No two people will agree on the how much money is needed to be **RICH**.

Is it: **$1 million? $2 Million? $10 million? $100 million?   MORE?**

In this book, $1 million of savings at retirement is used as a baseline. If your wants and needs are more, or you cannot afford the baseline, just multiply the baseline $1 million by 1/2, 2, or 3, or whatever to serve your needs and wants.

The goal of this book is to enable the reader to have saved **at least $1 million** at retirement. The reader can then take the take the $1 million, **invest it** tax free at to 10 percent as explained in this book, and thus have tax-free income of $100,000 per year to **live on and enjoy without using the accrued $1 million in savings**!

1.2. WAYS TO GET RICH.

There are many ways you can to get rich. Here are some of the main ways:

a.   Inheriting or otherwise being given a million dollars or more.

b.   Inheriting or otherwise being given valuable property: jewels, stock, businesses, real estate, etc.

Unfortunately, not everyone is blessed with wealthy parents and or large inheritances so other options are needed:

c. Starting and owning a highly profitable business.

d. Engaging in highly profitable but illegal activities. (These are dangerous to your health, freedom, and life and are not recommended.)

e. Working in a daily job: Waiter, fast food, barber, beautician, sales person, doctor, lawyer, teacher, engineer, physicist, stockbroker, realtor, stock investor, real-estate investor, etc. Most readers may find simply working in a daily job no matter how much it pays is the only the path to riches for them. That's what this book is about.

Some jobs don't pay very much. Don't let that deter you. Some pay many, many times more than others. However much you earn, if you work, and only make minimum wage, you can become RICH by using Elmo's method.

If you make lots of money and still can't seem to accumulate enough money to be RICH, Elmo's method is for you too.

All the ways to get RICH listed in **a through e** above establish a source of wealth which, if properly managed, can develop a continuing stream of wealth enabling you to live a happy and prosperous life.

If you don't have a lot of money, this book will tell you how to get it (Elmo's method). If you have money or once you get it, this book will tell you how to keep and multiply it.

2. HOW TO GET RICH – ELMO'S METHOD!

2.1. PAY YOURSELF FIRST.

If you are not rich, step one is to get an income. For most everyone that means to **GET A JOB!** If you are able, get an advanced education and become a professional. Otherwise, get the best job available. Even with a very modest income, you are on your way to being rich. Elmo never made much money sorting mail on a train but he became RICH!!

Now that you are working, you have to pay your bills: rent, food, auto, insurance, clothes, etc. What do you pay first? **PAY YOURSELF FIRST!!!!!!!!!!!!** Who is the most important person in the world? **IT'S YOU** (and your spouse and children). What's most important? Your financial future! What if you don't have enough money to pay both yourself and your bills? **PAY YOURSELF FIRST!!!!!!!!!!** Read on……

But **UNDERSTAND,** you are going to become rich in most cases **BY INVESTING** not only **YOUR SAVINGS** but also **BORROWED MONEY.** To borrow money at the best interest rate, you must have a **SPOTLESS CREDIT RATING.** Always pay all your bills on time –

Never Never Never Be Late!!!!

How much should you pay yourself? **PAY YOURSELF AND INVEST at least 10 percent of your gross (before tax) income. IF POSSIBLE, AT LEAST $100 PER WEEK!!!!!**

What about your bills**? First, stop spending money you don't have. Pay off your bills! Get two jobs, three jobs - do whatever you have to. Don't ever be late paying a bill – it will ruin your precious credit rating. You can't get rich without a spotless credit rating. Pay off high interest bills first, then the lower interest ones.**

America is on its way to a minimum wage of $15 per hour. That's $600 per week, $2600 per month. If you make $10 per hour, that's $400 per week - not quite enough for 10 percent to be $100 per week so what should you do**? If you make $400 per week, invest at least $40 per week and more if possible. If you make $600 per week, invest at least $60 per week and more if possible.**

DO WHATEVER IS NECESSARY TO PAY YOURSELF FIRST – TARGET AT LEAST $100 PER WEEK – THAT'S WHAT ELMO DID!!! Live with your parents or relatives. Eat at Home! Get a roommate to share expenses. Get a spouse. **DO WHATEVER YOU HAVE TO DO!** But, don't ever be an equal partner with anyone else. **DON'T EVER LOSE CONTROL!!!** More about that later! A spouse is different. A spouse is a legal relationship – a property settlement agreement will decide how things are divided upon divorce.

BUT NO MATTER WHAT, PUT 10 PERCENT – TARGET AT LEAST $100 PER WEEK ($433.33 PER MONTH, $5200 PER YEAR) - IN YOUR INVESTMENT ACCOUNT STARTING IMMEDIATELY! PUT IN MORE OR LESS IF YOU MAKE MORE OR LESS.

2.2. COMPOUND INTEREST IS PATH TO RICHES.

Assume that you have $100 per week ($433.33 per month, $5200 per year) to invest. How much will your investment increase if you invest it at a return of 10 percent compound interest per year? By the way, $100 per week is 10 hours work per week (or 5 hours each per week for a couple) at a minimum wage of $10 per hour.

Go on internet to find an investment calculator and see how it was used to fill in the below table. If you haven't done this before, you will find the results absolutely amazing and life changing. Here are the facts:

INVESTING $100 PER WEEK
AT 10 PERCENT INTEREST COMPOUNDED MONTHLY

YEAR	$CUMULATIVE AMOUNT INVESTED	$CUMULATIVE INTEREST @ 10 %	$CUMULATIVE INVESTMENT VALUE
1	5200	287	5487
10	52000	37,440	89,440
20	104000	227,555	331,555
30	156000	830,968	986,968

WOW! An investment of $100 per week at 10 percent compound interest per year will be worth

ONE MILLION DOLLARS in 30 years!!!!!

AN INVESTMENT OF $50 PER WEEK WILL BE WORTH **$500,000.**

All right, the total on the above chart is very slightly less than $1 Million. Putting in another $1.32 per week will make it worth more than a Million DOLLARS!

THE EXTRA $1.32 PER WEEK WILL BE WORTH $13,032 IN 30 YEARS.

OOPS! You have just earned $830,968 in Interest! The tax collectors (Federal and State) are poised to collect income tax wiping out a great portion of your interest earnings – **UNLESS YOU TOOK ACTION 30 YEARS BEFORE TO AVOID TAXES AS EXPLAINED IN SECTION 4.**

Where and how can you get compound interest at 10 percent per year?

That's the story in much of the rest of this book.

- **Residential Real Estate**
- **Rental Real Estate**
- **Tax Avoidance**
- **IRA and ROTH**
- **Employer Matching Funds**
- **Tax Free Exchanges**
- **Mergers**

Last but not least. Maybe - First and Foremost!
- **Stock Market**

3. MANAGE AND INCREASE YOUR WEALTH – DON'T WORK AT IT! MANAGERS DON'T WORK!

In my youth, when I became a manager at Hughes Aircraft Company in Culver City, California, I was sent to their **Manager Training Program**. It was taught by Management Consultant Dr. Cyril O'Donnell.

His first lecture was that, "I was no longer a technical specialist, I was a Manager." My job was now to:

> **PLAN, ORGANIZE, DIRECT, AND CONTROL THE WORK OF OTHERS.**

Dr. O'Donnell next showed the movie, "Bridge on the River Kwai." It starred Alex Guinness as a captured British Officer Lt. Col. Nicholson. If you haven't seen it, do so! It shows the difference between managers and workers. As the movie points out:

> **"OFFICERS DON'T WORK!"**

If you have implemented Elmo's method, as explained in **Section 2**, you are now the **CEO (Chief Executive Officer)** of what will become a million dollar company.

Your job is now to:

> **PLAN, , ORGANIZE, DIRECT, AND CONTROL the work and efforts of those who will carry out work for you that is necessary to make you rich.**

ALONG WITH PUTTING OTHERS (USUALLY EXPERTS) TO WORK FOR YOU, TO BECOME RICH IT IS ALSO NECESSARY TO USE THE MONEY OF OTHERS AND PUT IT TO WORK FOR YOU. THIS MEANS BORROWING THEIR MONEY AND PAYING INTEREST ON IT AS LONG AS YOU HAVE IT. REMEMBER, YOU CAN'T BORROW MONEY UNLESS YOU HAVE A SPOTLESS CREDIT RATING.

4. STAY RICH!! MAKE SURE YOUR INVESTMENTS ARE NO TAX OR LOW TAX:

4.1. GENERAL TAX RULES.

NOTE: The following material contains information about taxes. It is believed to be accurate. However, you may have nuances and situations that should be reviewed and checked with the IRS tax guides or reviewed by qualified tax software or specialists.

In general, taxes are simple:

*   If you have income in the form of wages, goods, or services, it is probably taxable.

* If you buy an item and use it to earn income, the income is probably taxable but the cost of the item is deductible. The item can be depreciated and its COST deducted from your income taxes over its useful life.

* If you buy something and sell it for more than you paid, then the increase is probably taxable, BUT NO TAX IS DUE UNTIL YOU SELL IT!!!!!

4.2. IRA.

An IRA is a great deal! Untaxed income (up to $5500 principle per year) can be invested. Taxes on the principle and income are deferred until withdrawn usually at retirement when your income is lower. If the IRS resumes a program to allow conversion of IRA funds to Roth by paying taxes on the IRA, do it – you may never get another chance.

4.3. ROTH.

A Roth IRA is even a better deal! !!!! AFTER-TAX INCOME (up to $5500 per year) can be invested in a ROTH.   THERE ARE NO TAXES ON PRINCIPLE OR ACCRUED INTEREST AT WITHDRAWAL. TAX-FREE PRINCIPLE AND TAX-FREE INCOME CAN BE WITHDRAWN USUALLY AT RETIREMENT.

There are other benefits of a Roth that are amazing, including passing any remaining principle and interest on to your heirs tax free.

Ask an On-Line Broker to open an IRA and a Roth for you. (See section 11.)

4.4. EMPLOYER MATCHING FUNDS IN RETIREMENT FUND.

This is another great deal if you can get it. Grab it. Your Employer's matching money is tax free to you in an IRA or Roth if you put up matching funds. Don't fail to take advantage of free money!

4.5. PERSONAL RESIDENCE – BUY, DON'T RENT!! YOU CAN DO IT TAX FREE.

 Home ownership is the largest source of wealth for most people.   Renting is money thrown away. You need a place to live, so pay yourself rent and use it to buy the property you are living in. Property taxes and mortgage interest paid on the property you buy are deductions from your income tax and will greatly reduce your income tax bill.   Insurance must be purchased but it is not income tax deductible.

THERE IS EVEN MORE GOOD NEWS. Real Estate values increase about 8 percent a year in good areas. Your house will be worth twice what you paid for it or more in about 10 to 15 years if it is in a good area and you maintain it in good condition.

THERE IS YET EVEN MORE GOOD NEWS ABOUT BUYING A PERSONAL RESIDENCE. Live in it for at least two years before you sell it and any **GAIN IN VALUE (PROFIT)** is **TAX FREE for a single person of up to $250,000 and for a joint return of up to $500,000!!!!** In general, real-estate prices go up every year. From a wealth standpoint, it is essential to buy a home rather than rent in most circumstances if you can and are willing to accept the responsibilities of home ownership. More people are born than die so home prices in most locations usually go up every year.

Sell your home tax free after you live in it at least two years. Buy another more expensive home using your current home for a down payment. For many investors, that's even better than the Tax-Free Exchanges described in the next **section**.

 Unfortunately, interest, taxes, and insurance on a personal residence increase commensurately with the value of your home. It doesn't make economic sense keep trading up in value to the extent that you can't afford pay the interest, taxes, and insurance to live in the residence while you are buying it. If you are reaching this plateau, it may be time to invest in rental real estate or other investments described in subsequent sections.

Many people who near retirement age, have their home paid for, and children grown up, then sell their home and use and invest its equity to retire. That, along with their pensions, Social Security, and Medicare makes for a very comfortable and secure retirement.

Many other people are content to just stay put, live out their lives in the same house, pay off their mortgage, and leave their home and its equity to their heirs to dispose of as their heirs see fit. It's up to you! As above, along with their pensions, Social Security, Medicare, and a paid-for home make for a very comfortable and secure retirement.

4.6. TAX-FREE EXCHANGES OF PROPERTY – LIKE KIND SWAPS: TAX-FREE INVESTING – TAX FREE EXCHANGES OF LIKE-KIND PROPERTY.

If you buy property, and later it has increased in value and you then sell it, you will owe tax on the profit. But if you exchange (trade) the investment property for a more valuable property, then no tax is due until you sell your new property. And if you repeat the process with another more valuable like property exchange, no tax is due on any gain of your exchange (trade) of like-kind property. Many, many people have become millionaires using this path to wealth in real estate and other like-kind investments.

4.7. STOCKS, SECURITIES, AND MUTUAL FUNDS.

Unfortunately there is no relief for the taxes on profits on money, securities, stocks, and mutual funds. If you buy, trade, or sell any of these, any gain is taxable and any loss is tax deductible. Whenever you sell (or buy) any of these, your Broker will send you a statement at the end of the tax year telling you and the IRS of any gains (or losses) and you must pay tax accordingly.

However, note the exceptions for IRAs (**section 4.2**), Roth's (**section 4.3**), and Employer Matching Retirement funds (**section 4.4**). If you invest in stocks, bonds, and other equities outside of these, when you sell, you will be immediately taxed on any gain (or loss).

So how can you avoid taxes on any of these? Easy, **JUST DON'T SELL THEM UNTIL YOU ARE READY TO RETIRE** and are thus in a low income phase of your life. Another way is to use a down period in stock markets to sell the losers and thereby deduct the losses or offset your losses against any gains to minimize total tax if winners are also sold.

5. INCREASING YOUR WEALTH: YOUR INVESTMENTS SHOULD GROW BY 8 10 TO 12 PERCENT PER YEAR!

How can investments grow without working at it full time? Put other people to work for you **(Section 3**).

6. NO MATTER WHAT THE SELLER PROMISES, IF IT'S NOT WRITTEN IN THE CONTRACT, IT DOESN'T EXIST.

When you buy a new home, you will have a **WRITTEN** home warranty. With a resale, you will have a **WRITTE**N home inspection. Make sure the inspector is licensed. If the seller makes a promise, put it in the sales contract.

Real Estate Agents, whether residential or commercial, work, on commission. Get to know an Agent who comes highly recommended to you. Let them know what you want. Explain you want to work with them long term for buying and selling several properties. Use a different set of eyes for buying and selling. Use one agent when buying property and a different agent for selling the same property later.

Unless you are an expert, you need to use licensed inspectors and appraisers for any property you contemplate purchasing or selling - whether diamonds or duplexes.

With stocks, mutual funds and the like, you can invest on your own as explained in **section 8** or use an Investment Advisor. It would seem that if you turn your money over to an Investment Advisor, then you will automatically become wealthy – much more so than if you invest on your own.   Unfortunately, Investment Advisors are not psychic and cannot always predict the future no matter how qualified they are. The Advisors certainly may become wealthy if they charge a flat fee or percentage of their clients' investments – they will get paid, no matter if their clients' investments increase or decrease. If you use an investment advisor, read the contract very carefully! The contract you sign is usually very clear that Advisor makes no representation as to the money you will make unless you are investing in equity such as a mortgage or loan with a fixed interest rate. But if the mortgage or loan isn't paid, even then, you still could lose substantially..

7. REAL-ESTATE "FLIPPING" HAS BECOME EPIDEMIC - PUT REAL-ESTATE AGENTS, FLIPPERS, AND OTHER PEOPLE'S MONEY TO WORK FOR YOU.

Don't expect to easily find a fixer-upper as someone probably has already grabbed the prime fixer upper residences or rentals for a quick profit with paint, new carpet, new appliances, and some landscaping. All the easily seen cosmetic defects have been fixed and the others hidden. Expensive furniture may have been rented and put in to make the home show better. Unfortunately, the flipper may have poor taste and you may have to redo all the supposed upgrades. House flipping extends from a $50,000 fixer-upper to a $200-million tear down. Check the Sunday Real Estate section of your newspaper, you will see very high-priced homes that have been flipped and flipped and then sold again in a short time.

In this day of insanely low real-estate mortgage interest rates, real estate prices are inflated over previous eras. Nevertheless, the low interest enables you to borrow other people's money at low rates and put it to work for you.

Real estate listing agents advise their clients to spruce up their home when it goes on the market so it will sell rapidly. Every real estate agent wants the property to be in tip-top condition so it will sell rapidly and produce maximum commission.

The above is not meant to disparage real estate agents or flippers. Put them to work for you. Good agents and good flippers do high quality upgrade and renovation work at a fair price. You are an investor. You are in for the long haul. But don't be taken in by cosmetic changes that mask problems. Your want high quality property at (or slightly below) fair market value - not an overpriced pig!

Flippers are now teaching flipping –it seems everyone is looking into flipping houses. Teaching flipping is a lucrative business and easier than actually flipping houses. You probably have received an invitation in the mail. Tickets to a "how-to-flip-houses" presentation are usually free but a book or package will probably be for sale at the presentation. There may be shills throughout the audience.

Remember, you are an investor, not a flipper. You are interested in buying high quality property at a fair price with a low-cost mortgage for the long haul for your residence or a rental.

8. REAL ESTATE – PERSONAL RESIDENCE.

A personal residence is a great first real estate investment. Rent you pay is gone forever. If you buy, your payments create equity in your investment.

Inspect the property yourself. Don't sign the purchase contract until all inspections have been completed, you have reviewed them, and all defects and discrepancies have been corrected.

After a few years or so, your personal residence will have appreciated, and you will have generated a significant down payment for a more expensive property. More important, you will have been able to learn about real estate investing, without the risk of investing in rental real estate.

For example, you may have bought a three-bedroom, one bath house as your first real estate investment. You intend to live in it for the next several years:

- Having only one bath, it was 30 years or so old and inexpensive compared to other potential purchases. Nevertheless, it was in a good neighborhood, in good shape, had a new roof, and didn't have termites or mold. The house though had a serious defect as it only had one bathroom. You were very very lucky to buy it as it seems in this day and age, every remodeler, real estate agent, and investor is a house-flipper.

- You worked with a remodeler **before you bought**! You made sure you could get a **Building Permit from the City. You checked with the City before you bought.** One of the bedrooms was divided into a second bathroom and a small bedroom. The small bedroom was large enough for a twin bed or a bunk bed.

- You made other improvements at minor cost: paint, carpet, new appliances.

Now, you may decide you are ready to step up and invest in the more demanding investments of rental real estate (**Section 9**). Or you may decide be your way of becoming wealthy is to move up to a bigger, more expensive personal residence in a better neighborhood every four to eight years while keeping your monthly payments affordable.

9. REAL ESTATE – RENTAL.

Many investors have written very good books on investing in **RENTAL** real estate. The most famous of these is:

> **How I Turned $1,000 into a Million in Real Estate in My Spare Time**
> by William Nickerson

Later versions address turning the $1000 into $3 and $5 Million. Reading Nickerson's book is a good way to start your career as the CEO of a Rental Real Estate Business.

The rental business is very simple and can be very profitable if you own enough rental properties. Start with a one family residence. Continue by selling and buying a two family rentals or a duplex. And so on. You may transition to business rental properties as well.

The value of rental property is determined by its **PROFIT:**

PROFIT = RENTAL INCOME LESS EXPENSES.

The seller of a rental property should be able to give you all this information for the last several years for you to evaluate. Your job as CEO of your rental business is to review the income and expense statements of a property you are interested in buying to determine if they are accurate and most important you can make 10 percent profit on you rental income.   Nickerson's books give detailed instructions about doing this.

Your next job is to determine how you might increase profits by raising rents: remodeling, landscaping, increasing security, etc. Perhaps the current rents are just too low and can be raised as a unit becomes available and the unit is redecorated.

Managing even one or two rentals or even a rental of a room in your personal residence requires a lot of knowledge. For example:

-Anything relevant to real estate must ordinarily be in writing signed by both parties. Verbal exchanges and changes to the written contract are not binding on either party.

- If there is a change to a written agreement, it must be in writing and signed by both parties.

- Take dated pictures of the property before a tenant moves in and after the tenant moves out.

- Always give written receipts and keep a copy of all receipts for rent, damage deposits, last month's rent, repairs, etc.

- Don't let tenants move in without paying all amounts due.

- Screen **ALL** tenants thoroughly in advance. Don't let a tenant move in without a through screening.   Some knowledgeable tenants are masters at gaming the rental system - **DO NOT RENT TO ONE**.

-

Once a tenant has moved in even if they have not yet paid rent, or if they never pay rent again, it may take a year or more to get them out while they game the eviction system, live rent free, and maybe extensively damage your property. There are businesses and on-line services that help tenants to avoid paying rent and avoid being evicted.

The solution is to put an expert to work for you by working with an experienced rental agent to handle all problems with tenants, rent collection, and eviction.

Make sure as well you work with the Homeowner Association and County regarding any permits for rentals and for building modifications or upgrades before you buy the rental property.

10. BUSINESS – GROW BY MERGER – BUT NEVER LOSE CONTROL!

As discussed in the previous sections, you are the CEO in the Rental Real Estate or other business you decide to enter. In most businesses, there is an economy of scale. If two businesses in a like endeavor merge, significant economies may be realized by:

- One telephone system instead of two.
- One rental agent instead of two.
- One answering service instead of two.
- One tax preparer instead of two.
- One office instead of two.
- Etc.

There are many more economies of scale. Every day that goes by is filled with business news that two companies have merged or one company has bought another company. Many of these are billion dollar mergers. The purpose is that the merged companies will be more profitable than the two companies separately.

Some mergers are friendly. Others are forced as one company bought the other company by controlling 50 percent of its stock.

No matter what your business, consider merger as a way to riches.

If you are a doctor with your own specially, consider merging with another doctor with a compatible specialty.

If you own a restaurant, merge with a bar.

The possibilities are endless.

But don't lose control. Suppose you merge with two other businesses, so there are three partners. One day you might wake up and find the other two partners have voted you out of the business!

11. INVESTING IN STOCK MARKET: STOCKS, MUTUAL FUNDS, AND EXCHANGE TRADED FUNDS (ETF).

"STOCK" MEANS A SHARE OF OWNERSHIP OF A COMPANY, MUTUAL FUND, OR ETF.
"MUTUAL FUND" MEANS A COMPOSITE THAT OWNS STOCK OF MANY CLOSELY RELATED COMPANIES.
"EXCHANGE-TRADED FUND (ETF)" ALSO MEANS A COMPOSITE THAT OWNS THE STOCK OF MANY CLOSELY RELATED COMPANIES.

If you own even only one share of a Mutual Fund or ETF, you actually own stock in all companies that Mutual Fund or ETF owns.

Shares of Stock in a COMPANY or an ETF can be bought or sold any time the Stock Market is open at current price. Mutual Funds can be bought and sold only at price at the end of the trading day.

Investing in stocks is the investment of choice for many. Investing in mutual funds or ETF that follow the major stock market indexes (Dow-Jones Industrial Average, Standard and Poor 500 index, etc) is easy and historically very profitable over the long term. Just what many investors who have a job are looking for (particularly if they enjoy their job). For example, to invest in rental real-estate, it helps to have a full time job or specialty closely related to real estate construction, remodeling, decoration, sales, or finance. The same situation applies to investing in stocks of a particular specialty.

Stock ownership is easy; you can buy stock and sell other stock you already own the same day.
NOTE: In this book, Charles Schwab is used as a typical Broker. Schwab is one of several very excellent low-cost Brokers. It's easy to OPEN an account to buy and sell stocks. You must be 18. Call, visit, or sign up on line with the Broker of your choice. There is probably an office near you. Open a ROTH Account, an IRA, and a Regular Account. Contact your bank and/or credit union to make internet deposits to and from your Brokerage accounts.

11.1. STOCK IS CERTIFICATE OF SHARE OF OWNERSHIP OF COMPANY.

If the owners want to sell part or all of a company to others, for example to pay debts or expand, their company can be divided into shares of ownership (Shares of Stock). The number of shares of stock in a single company may vary from 1 to billions of equal shares.

The original owner(s) of the company then allocate the company ownership by dividing the stock, usually keeping perhaps the majority according to their entitlement, and then selling the rest on the open market.

Before computers, actual printed and signed share certificates were issued, but in the electronic age, physical stock certificates are rarely issued.

The stock holders then elect the company's Board of Directors to run the company based on 1 vote for every share of stock owned.

The Board of Directors then appoints the company's Chief Executive Officer (CEO) and other company executives to run the company.

The following are the major Indexes which track the buying and selling of individual Stocks, Exchange Traded Funds (ETF), and Mutual Funds showing typical Daily and Year To Date (YTD) values:

	Daily Close	Daily Cng	Daily % Cng	YTD % Cng
Dow-Jones Industrials	17,535.39	+19.66	+0.11	+0.63
Standard and Poor (S&P) 500	2,037.05	+1.11	+0.05	-0.34
Standard and Poor 400	1,418.35	+4.49	+0.32	+1.41
Russell 2000	1.080.23	+0.69	+0.06	-4.90
Nasdaq	4,766.79	-6.72	-0.14	-4.81
Nikkei	17,134.37	+242.04	+1.43	-9.98
HangSeng HongKong	20,345.61	-269.62	-1.31	-7.16

For example, the S&P 500 Index tracks a composite the stocks of 500 different high-quality companies. An investor can buy shares of an ETF or mutual fund that tracks this index. Two of several are Vanguard S&P 500 EFT (trading symbol "voo") and Schwab S&P 500 Mutual Fund (trading symbol swppx). (**See section 11.8**.)

If you were to buy shares (or even a portion of a share) of voo or swppx, you would own some of the stock of all the companies in the S&P 500 index. Standard and Poor (S&P) and Vanguard (or Schwab) would charge a very, very small commission on the transaction.

Comparing these indexes with each other is very important. For example, the bottom two indexes are of foreign countries. They are down much more than the top five American indexes, showing that the foreign economies are lagging America's economy.

Also, very, very important, if one of the four American indexes suddenly takes a major dive (or makes a sudden increase), it may portend serious Trouble (or Good News) is ahead for the American economy. In this case, it is necessary to determine the cause of the sudden change and take any necessary action.

11.2. AS INVESTOR, YOUR GOAL SHOULD BE FOR EACH SHARE OF STOCK YOU OWN TO INCREASE IN VALUE BY 10 PERCENT EVERY YEAR.

– THAT'S THE GOAL OF 10 PERCENT COMPOUND INTEREST IN SECTION 2.2.

If you invest in **1** share, at a cost of **$100**, it should be worth **$110** at the end of 1 year. At the end of year **2,** it should be worth **$121**, and so forth.

AS SHOWN IN SECTION 2.2, IF YOU INVEST $100 PER WEEK FOR 30 YEARS at 10% COMPOUND INTEREST, IT WILL BE WORTH:

ONE MILLION DOLLARS!!!!

For example, to buy a **STOCK of a Company, MUTUAL FUND,** or **ETF,** log on to your Brokerage Account. Suppose you want to buy $1000 of S&P 500 Mutual Fund **swppx or** ETF **voo,** or **Total Stock Market ETF vti**.   These funds consist of stocks that track the composition of the largest and most profitable companies. **See Section 11.8.** Over the years, the value of these funds on average increases from 8 to 12 % per year**. JUST WHAT YOU NEED!**

 Based on past performance, **IF YOU INVEST $100 PER WEEK TOTAL IN voo, vti** AND/OR **swppx YOU WILL HAVE CLOSE TO $1 MILLION IN 30 YEARS.**

JUST WHAT WE ARE LOOKING FOR!!!

Investing in mutual funds or exchange traded funds ETF), enables you to own hundreds of stocks in each fund. This minimizes what would be a catastrophic loss if you own only a few stocks and one stock tanks. On the other hand, if you are a sophisticated investor and pick a big winner such as Apple (symbol aapl), you might become a millionaire in only a few months.

11.3. INVESTING IN STOCKS OF SPECIFIC COMPANIES.

STOCK IS BOUGHT TO MAKE MONEY for its investor. It does this by: PAYING DIVIDENDS AND APPRECIATING IN VALUE!

As with mutual funds and ETF, as an investor you should strive for your stock market stocks to increase in value by 10 percent each year. This means that the associated company must grow and make adequate profit each year.

Some of the profit a company makes is distributed to stockholders as periodic dividends. Some is invested in making the company grow so it can make more profit the next year.

The gauge of how well a company is earning profit is measured by its earnings. Its earnings must be adequate to pay the expenses of the company and significant profit.

Stockholders are not interested in a company that does not make profit. There is no return for their investment of buying and owning stock. A company may stay in business and earn enough to pay its employees, managers, and other expenses, but if there is no profit for the stockholders, the company executives are soon fired and replaced. In extreme cases, if there is not turnaround in company performance, the share holders vote to dismantle the company, sell its components, and divide the funds from the sale among the shareholders.

There is an important relationship between the price per share (**P**) of a company's stock and its earnings per share (**E**). Its Price per Share (**P**) divided by its estimated annual Earnings per share (**E**) is its **P/E**. For example if the price for a share of stock is $100 and its earnings per share are $10, its P/E is 100/10 = 10. The share price (**P**) is expected to increase as investors flock to this attractive P/E. A profitable company with good earnings (**E**) will pay a dividend to the stock holders and invest some of its profit it into expanding.

The next year, the growing company's stock price may rise to $110 and its earnings to $11 so its new P/E would be: $110/$11 = 10.
That is just the kind of stock to invest in to give a 10% growth per year of our investment.

The average P/E of companies on the New York Stock Exchange is about 13.

If the P/E of a growing company decreases for example from 13 to 10, investors would rush to buy it forcing up the share price and increasing the P/E to perhaps 12.

DON'T GET ENAMORED BY P/E. GET ENAMORED BY E!!!!!!

**REMEMBER IT'S A COMPANY'S EARNINGS PER SHARE (E) THAT ARE IMPORTANT!!!
EARNINGS PER SHARE (E) SHOULD BE INCREASING BY ABOUT 8 TO 12 PERCENT OR MORE PER YEAR.
THIS WILL DECREASE THE P/E AND INVESTORS WILL INVEST IN THE STOCK FORCING UP THE PRICE PER SHARE INCREASING THE P/E. THIS IS ALL GOOD NEWS FOR THE INVESTOR EVEN THOUGH THE P/E THEN INCREASES.**

HOWEVER, TAKE THE CASE OF A STOCK FOR WHICH EARNINGS TAKE A DIVE. NATURALLY, THE LOWER EARNINGS WILL INCREASE THE P/E OF THE STOCK PERHAPS TO 30. INVESTORS WILL FLEE THE STOCK FORCING THE STOCK PRICE WAY DOWN AND DECREASING P/E!!!!!

INVEST IN COMPANIES WITH EARNINGS THAT INCREASE SUBSTANTIALLY YEAR AFTER YEAR WITH A P/E OF 8 TO 14.

**It's easy to compute the total earnings (T) of a company. Just multiply the total number of shares (S) of a company by its Earnings per Share (E):
  T = ES.**

11.4. SELECTING STOCKS, MUTUAL FUNDS, AND EXCHANGE TRADED FUNDS (ETF).

Picking and investing in a SPECIFIC STOCK is a detailed and risky task. START BY BUYING ONE Of MANY BOOKS ON INVESTING IN THE STOCK MARKET.

A good stock in a company such as Apple or Facebook, may go up 50% or much more in just few days. It might also go down 50% or much more in just a few minutes if its profit does not meet expectations.

Mutual funds and ETF, however, own many, many stocks in many many companies so if one stock tanks, it makes barely a ripple in fund price. On the other hand, the mutual fund and ETF follow the broad market so if there is a wide spread depression, the entire market can go down rapidly by 3 or 5 percent or more in a day. If you own a few mutual funds and ETF's you can sell them quickly if necessary. If you own dozens of individual stocks, it may take much longer to identify what action you should take and to do it.

Thus for most investors in the stock markets, the major portion of their investment should be in a few mutual funds and ETF. Some typical mutual funds and ETF to be considered are listed in section 11.8. The broad market indexes in general average an increase of 7.5 to 12.5 per year. However, the specific swings in any specific year may be wider. So an investor could just pick a two or three of these funds and just keep investing week after week, month after month, and year after year and would probably average a 10 percent compound interest gain. Just what is needed!!! However, read sections 11.5 and 11.6 very carefully.

11.5. INVESTING IN STOCKS FOR LONG TERM (15 -30 YEARS).

If you are investing for the long term, and you are investing a broad coverage fund such as swpxx, voo, and vti, you should not be overly concerned about swings in fund valuation. If the fund goes up, you are happy making wonderful gains in your previously bought shares of your investment to date. If the fund goes down, you are happy because the price of the fund has fallen and you are buying lots of shares now at a low price!!!

Nevertheless, the common mistakes (**section 11.7**) should be danger signs for even a long term investor, who should be ready to get out of the market that is down and approaching ten percent loss in value.

11.6. INVESTING FOR SHORT TERM (5 -10 YEARS).

If you are investing in the stock market for the short term (**section 11.5**), you have a special problem. You may have been investing for 15 or 20 years or so, and have accumulated a substantial amount of gain from you investments – perhaps $500,000 or more. Your outlook is significantly different now. You can't afford to lose 50 percent of your capital if the market tanks. In this case it is prudent to get entirely out of the market if your investment falls 7 to 10 percent. Don't wait too long. Set a floor and stick to it.

If you investment is at $500,000, it's much better to get out with $475,000 than wait and get out with only $275,000. NOW IS THE TIME TO CONTINUE MAKING YOUR SMALL WEEKLY INVESTMENTS WHILE PRICES OF STOCK ARE LOW BUT HOLDING ON TO THAT $475,000.

When is the right time to reinvest the $475,000 that you have been holding out of the market? Even experts don't know the answer. Sometimes, if the market drops 10%, it will recover quickly. Sometimes, it will drop 10%, then quickly drop another 10%, and then seem to recover and then drop another 10%, perhaps more than 30 % or more. This is exactly what you wanted to avoid when you got out of the market. How do you proceed? It's up to you to decide determined by the amount of risk you want to take. It's a tough call for anyone.

One way to proceed is, "If the market seems to be recovering, make small investments of $500 or so from your capital along with your regular weekly investment."

Continue and perhaps increase the amount you invest periodically as long as the market is recovering, so as to be fully invested when the market recovers to the point where you exited. Don't stay out too long.

11.7. COMMON MISTAKES MADE BY STOCK INVESTORS.

* Holding a stock or fund that goes down too long. If the broad market as measured by the Dow-Jones Industrial Average or the S&P 500 goes down 10 percent, it significant bad news. If the market is down 20% it is a full-fledged "Bear" Market!

* Ignoring bad news of any kind including if one of the major indexes is out of step with the others. Ignoring wide spread erosion of Earnings.

* Ignoring any irregularities: CEO replacement, investigations, unexplained changes, etc.

* Becoming emotional about a stock or stock sector. For example, if computer stocks tank because of new technology, get out and stay out – they may (will) never come back to profitability.

* Staying out of a down market too long.

* Ignoring P/E and forward P/E showing earnings are not meeting expectations.

* Ignoring the Federal Reserve raising interest rates above the currently historically low rates. As interest rates rise, investors will move money out of stocks into "safe" bonds and other (safe) interest bearing investments. Companies cannot borrow money at low rates for expansion so P/E increases. Consumers cannot buy as much due to the higher interest rates reducing the earnings of companies.

* Ignoring:

- Financial crises in other countries (China, Greece, etc.)

- Rate of inflation increases making stock dividends less valuable.

- P/E rates (historically at about 14 for a stock or average for a mutual fund or ETF) rise to 20 or 30.

- Index of US Leading Economic Indicators turns down for several consecutive months.

- Only a few big stocks are pushing the market indexes higher. The Dow-Jones and S&P 500 Indexes are going higher but the indexes for smaller companies such as the Russell 2000 are not. This is bad news for the stock market as the market advance is not broad, the economic conditions are not broad based and a recession is around the corner. The large and small companies should be tracking together to show a broad based economic increase which will lead to an increase in stock prices.

11.8.   TYPICAL STOCK SYMBOLS, NAMES, AND ATTRIBUTES.

Log on to your Brokerage Account. Go to the "Research" section. The examples below provide typical examples for the reader of performance information available there. The reader should review the current online information and make investment decisions accordingly.

EXAMPLES below are accurate as of March, 2016.

Note: Items marked * might be determined by the reader to rate higher for consideration for investment. All investment items and those identified by the reader should be reviewed by the reader for possible investment using the latest on-line information. See section 11.2.

MUTUAL FUNDS

cgmfx   CGM Focus: Invests in 20 to 100 companies of about $5 billion in size.
Share price: $35.18   Rating: 1 Star. (Poor Performance)

gthix   Invesco Global Health: Invests in global health care companies.
Share price: $32.69   Rating: 2 Stars (Poor Performance)

hfgax   Henderson Global Technology: Invests in technology companies.
Share price: $22.06   Rating: 3 Stars (Poor Performance)

matfx   Mathews Asia Science and Technology: Invests in technology companies.
Share price: $11.39   Rating: 2 Stars (Poor Performance?)

rogsx* Red Oak Technology: Invests in technology companies.
Share price: $16.55   Rating: 4 Stars

ssaix* SSgA International: Invests in foreign companies.
Share price: $9.67   Rating: 4 Stars

swppx*Charles Schwab S&P 500: Tracks the total return of the highly respected and closely watched Standard and Poor (S&P) 500 Index. At least 80 percent of its stock holdings are in the S&P 500 Index.
Share price: $31.59   Rating: 4 Stars

gtlox* Glenmede Large Cap: Seeks maximum return consistent with reasonable risk by investing in large and medium size companies
Share price: $21.66   Rating: 5 Stars

EXCHANGE TRADED FUNDS

voo*   Vanguard 500: Tracks the performance of large capitalization stocks of the S&P 500 Index by replicating the stocks that make up the index.
Share price: $186.30 Rating: 4 Stars

vti*   Vanguard Total Market: Tracks the performance of large, medium and small capitalization stocks of the US Stock Market traded on the New York Stock Exchange and Nasdaq.
Share price: $103.32 Rating: 4 Stars

STOCKS

aapl	Apple Inc.	P/E: 11.22	Forward P/E: 11.65
	Share price: $105.67	Rating: 4 Stars (Good Earnings)	

Note: The above price $105.67 for aapl (Apple) was in March 2016. On May 1, 2016, Apple released an earnings report that showed a loss for the three-month quarter ending April 30, 2016. This was Apple's first loss in 13 years. As a result, its share price plunged. Price on May 11, 2016: $90.22 – a loss per share of $15.45 (15 percent).

Much more bad news about Apple's earnings is expected, but Apple is working hard to develop new profitable projects. This is an example of why diversified investments are necessary so as to be able to absorb a single catastrophic loss.

bac*	Bank of America Corp.	P/E: 10.61	Forward P/E: 9.58
	Share price: $13.68	Rating: 4 Stars (Poor Earnings?)	
fit	fitbit Inc.	P/E: 27.68	Forward P/E: 12.94
	Share price: $13.68	Rating: 2 Stars (Poor Earnings)	
luv*	Southwest Airline Co.	P/E: 13.57	Forward P/E: 10.43
	Share price: $44.06	Rating: 3 Stars (Good Earnings)	
rdn	Radian Group Inc.	P/E: 10.35	Forward P/E: 7.70
	Share price: $11.75	Rating: 3 Stars (Poor earnings?)	

11.9. DEVELOP A DIVERSIFIED INVESTMENT PLAN FOR MAXIMUM RETURN AT MINIMUM RISK.

Owning four investments in four different categories is better than owning only one investment if that one investment loses money.

Certainly, owning only one investment that makes lots money is best of all. However, if you own only one investment late in life and it loses lots of money, your retirement plans could be ruined as there aren't 20 or 30 years for you to recover.

The best strategy is to own a diversified portfolio of several (seemingly) very good investments in several categories. If one doesn't turn out very good, then the other investments will still be enough to provide the returns you want and balance out the losses of the poor performer.

Through all your investment activities, stay aware of the principles of investing for the long term (section 11.5), the short term (section 11.6), and common mistakes made by investors (section 11.7).

This section describes the development of a diversified investment plan that aims to create an annual average return of 8 to 12 percent over the long term. There is no guarantee here only the past performances of 8 to 12 percent gain by the major indexes (section 11.1) over the last 30 years or so. Sometimes they were up big, sometimes down big but over the long term the trend is upward. For more detailed information about what to expect, check the performance of the various major stock indexes yourself.

Here are some guidelines:

1. Invest in mutual funds or ETF (Exchange Traded Funds) that track the major averages.

2. Invest in companies that have Earnings increasing by about 10 percent every year. After all, that's what you want your investments to do – increase by 10 percent each year. Remember, it's EARNINGS that are important, NOT PE. A stock can have a good PE with poor earnings as everyone sells the stock which drives its Price down and its P/E down as well.

3. Invest in stocks that have a P/E (Price/Earnings) of about 8 to 14, with a FP/E (Forward P/E) moving down toward 10. Remember: if Price of a stock increases, P/E increases and a stock may not be worth the increased price. If Earnings increase, P/E goes down and the stock is a more valuable. Unfortunately, if Earnings go down, and investors dump the poorly performing stocks so its Price goes down, then the P/E may actually go down. So whenever buying or holding a stock, make sure its EARNINGS are going up and that is what is going on when a P/E is in a comfortable range.

4. Develop a diversified portfolio of investments.

The following sections will give you practice in doing so.

Sections 11.9.1 and 11.9.2 provide examples of a diversified list of stocks, mutual funds, and Exchange Traded funds that are potential investments. Use these sections as examples. Add to the lists yourself. Fill in the missing data of any entries of interest to you. Check and update the data.

The data changes rapidly so do not rely on the data in these charts. Go on your Broker's internet site to obtain the latest data.   The data in these charts is for example purposes only.

Develop your own DIVERSIFICATION SUMMARY list using the worksheet at the end of this section. If you select entries from the lists in sections 11.9.1, section 11.9.2, check them out yourself. Add to the list those you have identified yourself. Enter and update all your entries on your DIVERSIFICATION SUMMARY WORKSHEET at the end of this section. (section 11.9.4).

There is no right number of entries on your DIVERSIFICATION SUMMARY WORKSHEET. If you are a new investor, enter perhaps about 6 to 10. Increase or decrease the number of items on the list to the number that you feel comfortable with. Keep the list up to date as you identify new investment possibilities.

In selecting investments, pay particular attention to the "6 Mo %" and "12 Mo %" columns. These columns tell the percent change in price of the potential investment over the last 6 months and last 12 months. FP/E is the Forward-looking Price per share/Earnings per share.

11.9.1. EXAMPLE 1 DIVERSIFICATION SUMMARY

SYMBOL	CATEGORY	RATING	FP/E	6 Mo %	12 Mo %
aapl	Technology	C	11.9	-14.0	-29.83
bac	Banking	1	10.4	-4.15	-3.89
cgmfx	Wide Spectrum	1		-8.57	-13.76
des	Small cap dividend	5		8.7	4.1
fdl	Morningstar© dividend	4		10.5	11.9
fit	Health & Fitness Devices	D	11.8	-14.9	-16.7
gthix	Health	2		-7.21	-17.43
gtlox	Large Cap Russell© 1000	5		2.03	-0.71
hfgax	Health	3		-7.09	-4.81
jaglx	Large Cap Russell© 1000	4		-7.78	-17.28
jagtx	Technology	3		2.51	0.34
lceix	Growth/Dividends, 25% foreign	5		6.83	11.15
luv	Southwest Airlines	C	9.89	-3.63	7.16
matfx	Large Cap Dividend	2		-5.60	-6.74
mtz	Construction (Like Alcoa)	B	16.8	5.72	6.2
rdn	Mortgage Insurance Services	B	7.76	-1.82	-7.31
rogsx	Technology	4		7.11	5.31
schd	Dividend Equity	5		5.86	4.87
sstr	Games	0	?	-70.97	-35.71
swppx	S&P 500© Index	4		3.52	1.69
tcmgx	Medium-size Companies	3		-1.01	-9.86
voo	S&P 500© Index	5		2.76	3.60
vti	CRSP Entire US Stock Market	4		2.91	-0.30
	NA = NOT AVAILABLE				
	Note: A and 5 are best ratings.				

Be careful to stay diversified! For example, in 2000 or so, there were many manufacturers of large computers. Your investment in associated computer mutual funds would double every year or so. Then technology leap-frogged and many computer companies went bankrupt, merged, or closed their doors. Your investment tumbled by 80 percent and NEVER recovered. The moral is that if you invest in heavily in mutual funds, ETFs, or stocks in a limited area, there may be a rapid decline from which values never recover.

On the other hand, broad-index mutual funds and ETF may provide adequate diversification so as to cushion the bumps in your investment road. For example, technology is changing right now, may quickly embrace 3D-holographic technology, and quickly drive out companies that can't keep up.

NOTE: When you buy or sell stocks, you must pay a "transaction" fee. Schwab, for instance, charges as fee of about $9.95 per stock transaction no matter how many shares are bought or sold. Make sure you understand the fee your broker will charge. This fee is always required for stock transaction. Many Mutual Funds and ETF transactions do not have a fee although some may have a fee of $50 or $100 or so. Again, make sure you know the fees you will be charged on specific mutual fund or ETF transactions.

Early in your investment activity, these fees may mount up quickly. So always check if there is a fee, and if it is significant, find an investment which does not require a fee.

11.9.2. EXAMPLE 2 DIVERSIFICATION SUMMARY

SYMBOL	CATEGORY	RATING	FP/E	6 Mo %	12 Mo %
c	Financial Services	C	9.66	-10.88	-14.69
cbs	Mass Media	B	13.32	6.30	5.69
f	Automotive/Mobility	A	6.33	1.39	-10.75
gnw	Mortgage Insurance	B	4.49	-0.56	-4.79
intc	Digital Technology	B	13.15	-2.77	0.75
jsvax	Equity Securities	2		-6.08	-17.09
kmi	Energy/Infrastructure/Pipelines	D	26.59	2.12	-21.87
maptx	Asian Companies Except Japan	4		1.19	-8.02
mpel	Casino Gambling/Entertainment	5	38.43	-1.66	-5.54
mtz	Construction/ Engineering	B	17.12	34.01	19.91
mu	Semiconductors	C	95.03	-15.94	-52.57
phm	Home Building/Mortgage Banking	F	12.01	6.9	-3.53
sgenx	Capital Growth	5		0.70	-4.75
spg	Real Estate	C	31.43	6.92	14.67
swhgx	Home Building/Mortgage Banking	F		3.15	-2.69
swssx	Russell 2000©	3		2.32	12.14
symc	Computer/Internet Security	D	15.38	15.53	-1.83
umbwx	Foreign Large Growth	3		2.80	-7.55
wfc	Banking	C	21.48	-14.62	-17.88
wgrnx	Underpriced Companies	3		-0.26	-3.79
wpg	Real Estate	B		2.57	-19.48
voya	Retirement/Insurance Services	B	9.39	-21.97	-38.61
	Note: A and 5 are best ratings.				

YOU NOW HAVE A DIVERSIFICATION SUMMARY WORKSHEET (section 11.9.4) listing your potential investments. Next, make an INVESTMENT ACTION PLAN (section 11.9.3) of your planned investments and how much to invest. If you will be making weekly investments, make one investment each week (or make monthly investments if that fits your schedule better). Continue for the next 30 years. An example INVESTMENT ACTION PLAN is shown in section 11.9.3

Document your plan in an INVESTMENT ACTION PLAN WORKSHEET at the end of this section (section 11.9.5).
From the Entries in the DIVERSIFICATION SUMMARIES (sections 11.9.1, 11.9.2, and your worksheet (section 11.9.4, prepare your INVESTMENT ACTION PLAN WORKSHEET (section 11.9.5). In the ACTION column, + indicates BUY, - indicates SELL.

It's worth the reader's time to review the DIVERSIFICATION SUMMARIES in sections 11.9.1 and 11.9.2 to understand why the investments on the EXAMPLE INVESTMENT ACTION PLAN (section 11.9.3) were chosen by the Author and are (were) in the Author's Portfolio. However, time has passed and there is no guarantee with these. It's up to the readers to select their investments themselves.

Always keep in mind: EARNINGS ARE WHAT BUSINESS IS ALL ABOUT! A BUSINESS IS WORTHLESS TO AN INVESTOR UNLESS IT MAKES EARNINGS THAT PAY EXPENSES, PROVIDE FUNDS FOR GROWTH, AND PROVIDE DIVIDENDS TO THE INVESTORS (OWNERS). P/E IS A MEASURE OF THE STOCK PRICE (P) TO EARNINGS (E). See section 11.3. Always check the P/E and FP/E before buying an investment to make sure it is not overpriced.

11.9.3. EXAMPLE INVESTMENT ACTON PLAN

SYMBOL/ ACCOUNT	AMOUNT $ OWNED	ACTION + or -	RATING	6 Month % Change	12 Month % Change
des sm cap div		+ 1000	5	8.7	4.1
fdl dividend		+1000	4	10.5	11.9
gtlox lg cap		+ 1000	5	2.03	-0.71
jagtx tech		+ 1000	3	2.51	0.34
lceix div& forgn		+ 1000	5	6.83	11.15
luv swair		+ 1000	C	-3.63	7.16
rogsx tech		+ 1000	4	7.11	5.31
schd dividend		+ 1000	4	5.86	4.87
swppx S&P	525	+ 1000	4	3.52	1.69
tcmgx medium			3	-1.01	-9.86
voo S&P		+ 1000	5	2.76	3.6
vti US mkt		+ 1000	4	2.91	-0.3
INVESTMENTS	525				
CASH	11000				Buy = +
TOTAL	11525	11000			Sell = -

11.9.4. DIVERSIFICATION SUMMARY WORKSHEET

SYMBOL	CATEGORY	RATING	FP/E	6 Mo %	12 Mo %
	Note: A and 5 are best ratings.				

11.9.5. INVESTMENT ACTION PLAN WORKSHEET   DATE:

SYMBOL/ ACCOUNT	AMOUNT $ OWNED	ACTION + or -	RATING	6 Month % Change	12 Month % Change
INVESTMENTS					
CASH					Buy = +
TOTAL					Sell = -

12. EPILOGUE.

ENJOY YOUR WEALTH!

The goal of this book has been to provide the reader a path to riches by making weekly investments over a 30 year period. This is done by paying yourself first. Pay yourself a 10 % portion of you weekly earnings to make periodic weekly investments in good opportunities of your choice as described in this book.

This type of investing is called "income averaging." In good times the price of investing trends higher but the previous investments increase in value commensurately. In tough times, the price of investing trends lower and the value of the previous investments may decrease, but the current periodic investment buys more than before.

Over the long term, the value of good investments increases, and as an added benefit, compensates for inflation as well.

Thus, the value of routine periodic investments may approach $1 million or more and will provide enough investment income after retirement to support almost any reasonable retirement need. In many cases, pensions from employment, Social Security, Medicare, and medical insurance from retirement plans will cover basic living expenses, so the principle of investment funds does not need to be used and could be available for heirs.

Regardless, how to spend you investment money at retirement is your choice – spend it to the last penny or save some for your heirs. ENJOY YOUR WEALTH!

John Gilbert Bean   johnGilbertBean@WordPress.com

Send comments to: JBeanMBean@msn.com

INDEX

www.ingramcontent.com/pod-product-compliance
Lightning Source LLC
Chambersburg PA
CBHW080551190526
45169CB00007B/2728